IMAGES OF WA

THE WARSAW UPRISINGS 1943-1944

RARE PHOTOGRAPHS FROM WARTIME ARCHIVES

Ian Baxter

Pen & Sword
MILITARY

First published in Great Britain in 2021 by
PEN & SWORD MILITARY
an imprint of
Pen & Sword Books Ltd
47 Church Street
Barnsley
South Yorkshire
S70 2AS

ISBN 978-1-52679-991-3

A CIP catalogue record for this book is available from the British Library.

Typeset by Concept, Huddersfield, West Yorkshire HD4 5JL
Printed and bound in England by CPI Group (UK) Ltd, Croydon CR0 4YY

Pen & Sword Books Limited incorporates the imprints of Atlas, Archaeology, Aviation, Discovery, Family History, Fiction, History, Maritime, Military, Military Classics, Politics, Select, Transport, True Crime, Air World, Frontline Publishing, Leo Cooper, Remember When, Seaforth Publishing, The Praetorian Press, Wharncliffe Local History, Wharncliffe Transport, Wharncliffe True Crime and White Owl.

For a complete list of Pen & Sword titles please contact
PEN & SWORD BOOKS LIMITED
47 Church Street, Barnsley, South Yorkshire S70 2AS, England
E-mail: enquiries@pen-and-sword.co.uk
Website: www.pen-and-sword.co.uk

Dedicated to the brave souls

who fought and died

during the Warsaw rebellions

Contents

About the Author

Ian Baxter is a military historian who specialises in German twentieth-century military history. He has written more than fifty books including *Poland – The Eighteen Day Victory March*, *Panzers In North Africa*, *The Ardennes Offensive*, *The Western Campaign*, *The 12th SS Panzer-Division Hitlerjugend*, *The Waffen-SS on the Western Front*, *The Waffen-SS on the Eastern Front*, *The Red Army at Stalingrad*, *Elite German Forces of World War II*, *Armoured Warfare*, *German Tanks of War*, *Blitzkrieg*, *Panzer-Divisions at War*, *Hitler's Panzers*, *German Armoured Vehicles of World War Two*, *Last Two Years of the Waffen-SS at War*, *German Soldier Uniforms and Insignia*, *German Guns of the Third Reich*, *Defeat to Retreat: The Last Years of the German Army At War 1943–45*, *Operation Bagration – the Destruction of Army Group Centre*, *German Guns of the Third Reich*, *Rommel and the Afrika Korps*, *U-Boat War*, and most recently *The Sixth Army and the Road to Stalingrad*. He has written over a hundred articles including 'Last days of Hitler', 'Wolf's Lair', 'The Story of the V1 and V2 Rocket Programme', 'Secret Aircraft of World War Two', 'Rommel at Tobruk', 'Hitler's War With his Generals', 'Secret British Plans to Assassinate Hitler', 'The SS at Arnhem', 'Hitlerjugend', 'Battle of Caen 1944', 'Gebirgsjäger at War', 'Panzer Crews', 'Hitlerjugend Guerrillas', 'Last Battles in the East', 'The Battle of Berlin', and many more. He has also reviewed numerous military studies for publication, supplied thousands of photographs and important documents to various publishers and film production companies worldwide, and lectures to various schools, colleges and universities throughout the United Kingdom and the Republic of Ireland.

Chapter One

Prelude

Following the German invasion of Poland in September 1939 the Nazi government quickly began incorporating large areas of Poland into the Reich. They cleared the Poles and Jews out and replaced them with German settlers. The unincorporated areas, comprising the provinces of Lublin and parts of Warsaw and Krakow, were known as the 'General Government'. They became the dumping ground for those deemed enemies of the state. It was here that the first deportations of Poles and Jews were sent in their thousands.

By early 1940 the Germans realised that simultaneously moving Poles, Jews and ethnic Germans had become an administrative nightmare, and it was agreed that the Jews would be forced to live in ghettos. Hundreds of ghettos were built to confine and segregate them. In smaller towns the ghettos often served as temporary holding areas, to use Jews for slave labour and later move them to larger ghettos.

The largest ghetto built was the Warsaw Ghetto, officially known by the Germans as the 'Jüdischer Wohnbezirk in Warschau' (Jewish Residential District in Warsaw).

On 1 April 1940, District Governor Ludwig Fischer ordered the construction of the ghetto wall. Built primarily by the Jews themselves, it was to completely encircle the ghetto.

On 2 October, Fischer issued the 'Regulations for Restrictions on Residence in the General Government of 13 September 1940'. It read:

1. A Jewish quarter is to be formed in the city of Warsaw, in which the Jews living in the city of Warsaw, or still to move there, must take up residence. The quarter will be set off from the rest of the city by the following streets: [here follows a list of streets and sections of streets].
2. Poles residing in the Jewish quarter must move their domicile into the other part of the city by 31 October 1940. Apartments will be provided by the Housing Office of the Polish City Hall. Poles who have not given up their apartments in the Jewish quarter by the above date will be forcibly moved. In the event of a forcible removal they will be permitted to take only luggage, bed-linen, and articles of sentimental value. Poles are not permitted to move into the German quarter.

3. Jews living outside the Jewish quarter must move into the Jewish area of residence by 31 October 1940. They may take only refugee luggage and bed-linen. Apartments will be allocated by the Jewish Elder.
4. The Appointed Mayor of the Polish City Hall and the Jewish Elder are responsible for the orderly move of the Jews to the Jewish quarter, and the punctual move of the Poles away from the Jewish quarter, in accordance with a plan yet to be worked out, which will provide for the evacuation by stages of the individual police districts.
5. The Representative of the District Governor of the city of Warsaw will give the necessary detailed instructions to the Jewish Elder for the establishing and permanent closure of the Jewish quarter.
6. The Representative of the District Governor of the city of Warsaw will issue regulations for the execution of this Decree.
7. Any person contravening this Decree, or the Regulations for its execution, will be punished in accordance with the existing laws on punishment.
Head of the Warsaw District, Dr. Fischer (Governor)

By 16 October 1940 the ghetto was officially in operation and imprisoned around 400,000 Jews.

As the ghetto became more established, the German authorities began various business enterprises, often for the war effort, using ghetto inhabitants for labour. Work was a welcome relief, as conditions inside the ghetto were soon appalling.

The Germans did nothing to alleviate hunger and disease. Epidemics became a feature of life along with starvation diets – 76,000 deaths recorded before July 1942.

At the Wannsee conference in January 1942, senior Nazi officials and SS leaders agreed that the ghettos should be 'liquidated'. This meant the Jews being deported from the ghettos and sent to the various labour and murder camps that were being built such as Auschwitz-Birkenau, Chełmno, Treblinka, Belzec and Sobibor.

The clearing of the Warsaw ghetto and transportation to the death camps was an immense undertaking. The first phase, called Grossaktion Warschau, was set in motion on 22 July 1942. The destination was TII, known to the SS as Treblinka.

In charge of the shipments was SS-Hauptsturmführer Hermann Höfle. He issued the following order to the Jewish Council in Warsaw:

1. All Jewish persons irrespective of age or sex who live in Warsaw will be resettled in the east.
2. The following are excluded from the resettlement:
   (a) All Jewish persons who are employed by the German authorities or by German agencies and can provide proof of it.
   (b) All Jewish persons who belong to the Jewish Council and are employees of the Jewish Council.

(c) All Jewish persons who are employed by German firms and can provide proof of it.

(d) All Jews capable of work who have not hitherto been employed. They are to be placed in barracks in the ghetto.

(e) All Jewish persons who are members of the personnel of the Jewish hospitals. Similarly, the members of the Jewish disinfection troops.

(f) All Jewish persons who belong to the Jewish police force.

(g) All Jewish persons who are close relatives of the persons referred to in (a)–(f). Such relatives are restricted to wives and children.

(h) All Jewish persons who on the first day of the resettlement are in one of the Jewish hospitals and are not capable of being released. The fitness for release will be decided by a doctor to be designated by the Jewish Council.

3. Every Jewish person being resettled may take 15kg of his property as personal luggage. All valuables may be taken: gold, jewellery, cash etc. Food for three days should be taken.

4. The resettlement begins on 22 July 1942 at 11 o'clock.

II. The Jewish Council is responsible for providing the daily quota of Jews for transportation. To carry out this task the Jewish Council will use the Jewish police force (100 men). The Jewish Council will ensure that every day from 22 July onwards, by 16.00 at the latest, 6,000 Jews will be assembled directly on the loading platform near the transfer office. To start with, the Jewish Council may take the quotas of Jews from the whole population. Later, the Jewish Council will receive special instructions according to which particular streets and blocks of flats are to be cleared.

VIII. Punishments:

(a) Any Jewish person who leaves the ghetto at the start of the resettlement without belonging to the categories of persons outlined in 2(a) and (c), and in so far as they were not hitherto entitled to do so, will be shot.

(b) Any Jewish person who undertakes an act which is calculated to evade or disturb the resettlement measures will be shot.

(c) Any Jewish person who assists in an act calculated to evade or disturb the resettlement measures will be shot.

(d) All Jews who, on completion of the resettlement are encountered in Warsaw and do not belong to the categories referred to in 2(a)–(h) will be shot.

The Jewish council is hereby informed that in the event that the orders and instructions are not carried out 100%, an appropriate number of the hostages who have been taken in the meantime will be shot.

For eight weeks, the liquidation action of transporting Jews from Warsaw to Treblinka continued daily via two shuttle trains, each carrying several thousand people. Some 265,000 ghetto residents were sent to the Treblinka extermination camp, and 20,000 were deported to labour camps. By the end of 21 September 1942, approximately 48,000 Warsaw Jews had died at Treblinka.

As a result of this first action, there had been growing underground activity of ghetto resistors who had learnt that the transports for 'resettlement' had led to mass killings. Reports received from western governments also confirmed that the inhabitants of the ghetto had been shipped to sites where they were exterminated. Fearing for their lives, many of the remaining Jews decided to resist.

Over the coming weeks and months the newly established underground fighters known as ZOB (Żydowska Organizacja Bojowa: Jewish Combat Organization) and ZZW (Żydowski Związek Wojskowy: Jewish Military Union) began smuggling in weapons, ammunition and supplies to resist the next liquidation operation.

This photograph taken in October 1941 shows Jewish men peering over the wall overlooking Mirowski Square that divided the Warsaw ghetto into the small and large ghettos. The apartment house in the background was located at 12 Krochmalna Street, which was the home of the person who took this image, Irving Milchberg. German authorities closed the Warsaw ghetto to the outside world on 15 November 1940. The wall around it was 3 metres high and topped with barbed wire. Occupants were shot on sight if they attempted to escape. German policemen from Battalion 61 held victory parties when a large number of escapees were shot at the ghetto wall. (*USHMM, Irving Milchberg*)

Ghetto residents make purchases from street vendors. This photograph is one of a series taken by German soldier Willy Georg. Georg served as a radio operator in the German army and supplemented his income by taking pictures of his fellow soldiers with his Leica camera. In summer 1941 when his unit was stationed in Warsaw, Georg was issued a pass by one of his officers and instructed to enter the enclosed ghetto and bring back photos of what he saw. He shot four rolls of film and began to shoot a fifth when he was stopped by a detachment of German police. Failing to check his pockets for finished rolls of film, the police confiscated only the film in his camera before escorting him out of the ghetto. (USHMM, Rafael Scharf)

A photograph taken by Willy Georg in the summer of 1941 showing a Jewish man riding in a rickshaw on a crowded street in the Warsaw ghetto. The ghetto was the largest of all the Jewish ghettos across occupied Europe. It was established in November 1940. (USHMM, Rafael Scharf)

(**Opposite, above**) Jews in the street in the Warsaw ghetto. By April 1941 an additional 50,000 Jews had been resettled in the ghetto from the western part of the city, 3,000 from its eastern part, and 4,000 from Germany. At its height 460,000 Jews were imprisoned in the ghetto. (*USHMM, Rafael Scharf*)

(**Opposite, below**) Jews mill around on a side street in the Warsaw ghetto. Density of population was acute with some 146,000 people crammed in per square kilometre. (*USHMM, Rafael Scharf*)

(**Above**) Jews gathered on the plaza at Zamenhofa and Nowolipki streets listen to an announcement on the public address system. (*USHMM, Rafael Scharf*)

Jews converse on a street in the Warsaw ghetto. Note the Star of David armband on the Jewish gentleman on the left. When the Jews entered the ghetto they were ordered to wear badges or armbands with a yellow Star of David.
(*USHMM, Rafael Scharf*)

Jews ride in a streetcar marked with a Jewish star in the Warsaw ghetto. (*USHMM, Rafael Scharf*)

Two destitute children on the cobblestone pavement in a square in the Warsaw ghetto – one of them may be unconscious or dead. Conditions in the streets were terrible. Epidemics became a major feature of life, along with starvation diets. (*USHMM, Rafael Scharf*)

(**Opposite, above**) A destitute young man lies in the middle of the pavement on a street in the Warsaw ghetto with a collection cup. *(USHMM, Rafael Scharf)*

(**Opposite, below**) Warsaw ghetto residents stare at a man who has collapsed in the street. With insufficient hygiene coupled with diseases and starvation, thousands of people began to die in the ghetto. Approximately 76,000 deaths had been recorded by July 1942. *(USHMM, Benjamin (Miedzyrzecki) Meed)*

(**Above**) Destitute Jews sit on a street corner in the Warsaw ghetto begging for assistance. *(USHMM, Rafael Scharf)*

(**Above**) A destitute father and his two children sit on the street in the Warsaw ghetto. With food and medical supplies in serious short supply by summer 1941 the death rate considerably increased. (*USHMM, Rafael Scharf*)

(**Opposite, above**) Deportation of the Jewish inhabitants inside the Warsaw ghetto begins. In this photograph Jews have been rounded up and walk to the assembly area. The liquidation of the Warsaw ghetto was an immense undertaking and would be undertaken in phases. Responsibility for the shipments from Warsaw in liaison with the railway authorities of the Ostbahn was that of SS-Hauptsturmführer Hermann Höfle. The first and major phase of the liquidation began on 22 July 1942. (*USHMM, Instytut Pamieci Narodowej*)

(**Opposite, below**) Another photograph showing Jews being escorted to an assembly area. The liquidation of the Warsaw ghetto was a massive deportation of 265,000 ghetto residents to the newly-opened Treblinka extermination camp and 20,000 to labour camps.

A long column of Jews who have been rounded up for deportation walk with their luggage along a street in the Warsaw ghetto. *(USHMM, Louis Gonda)*

Jews crowding at the Umschlagplatz Square in the ghetto waiting to be transported to an extermination camp. *(Yad Vasham)*

Two photographs showing Jews assembled for deportation at the Umschlagplatz in the Warsaw ghetto.
(*USHMM, Instytut Pamieci Narodowej and Yad Vashem*)

Following the first deportation phase of the Warsaw ghetto in the summer of 1942, this photo depicts the transportation of Jews that have been loaded onto freight cattle cars bound for a concentration camp.

Chapter Two

The Jewish Ghetto Uprising 1943

German civilian and military authorities were torn between the removal of the Jewish communities from the ghettos and retaining their labour. They had employed considerable amounts of Jewish labour for their lucrative businesses. Following the first liquidation action, textile production had decreased by 50 per cent. By the end of 1942 only 60,000 Jews remained. With this in mind, when Himmler toured the ghetto on 9 January 1943 he grudgingly ordered Globocnik to remove just 8,000 more Jews. Those that remained, including their families, were regarded as 'essential workers'. The rest were subsequently sent to Treblinka and murdered.

So it was much to the surprise of the remaining Jewish community that on 18 January 1943 the second phase of the liquidation began. German units entered the ghetto and the inhabitants were called to file in the courtyards to present their papers for inspection. However, not everyone responded to the order. Most went into hiding, prepared to fight with their collection of handguns, petrol bottles, and various other weapons smuggled into the ghetto by resistance fighters. They knew they would not be able to defend themselves for long; it was a 'battle of honour', and a protest against a 'world of silence'.

A series of heavy exchanges of shooting in some sectors of the ghetto was followed by close quarter fighting. Ambushes had been laid for the Germans inside some of the houses, and those that entered were shot.

Both sides had suffered losses, but by 22 January the revolt had been stopped and the ghetto was back under German control. However, only 5,000 Jews had been rounded up, and this included patients from the ghetto hospital along with several members of the Judenrat – the Jewish administrators of the ghetto imposed by the Nazis. They were all assembled in the Umschlagplatz and then deported by train to Treblinka.

Though the rebellion had been contained, the German authorities were concerned. It was the first time the Jews had rebelled using arms against the authorities. For this reason Himmler was determined that the Warsaw Ghetto be liquidated as quickly as possible, in spite of the labour policy on war production. In February 1943 Himmler sent a letter:

Reichsführer SS Field Command
February 16, 1943. Secret!
To: Higher SS and Police Leader (Hoeher SS- und Polizeiführer),
     East SS Obergruppenführer Krueger, Kracow
For reasons of security I herewith order that the Warsaw Ghetto be pulled down after the concentration camp has been moved: all parts of houses that can be used, and other materials of all kinds, are first to be made use of.

The razing of the ghetto and the relocation of the concentration camp are necessary, otherwise we would probably never establish quiet in Warsaw, and the prevalence of crime cannot be stamped out as long as the ghetto remains.

An overall plan for the razing of the ghetto is to be submitted to me. In any case we must achieve the disappearance from sight of the living-space for 500,000 sub-humans that has existed up to now, but could never be suitable for Germans, and reduce the size of this city of millions – Warsaw – which has always been a centre of corruption and revolt.
Signed H. Himmler

The liquidation of the ghetto was planned for 19 April, the eve of the Passover, and its objective was to remove everyone within three days.

SS-Oberführer Ferdinand von Sammern-Frankenegg, who had been in charge of the first liquidation of the Warsaw ghetto in 1942, was also tasked with the last. However, this time the Jewish people were aware of their impending fate; they knew that it was not just a 'resettlement action'. The ŻZW and ŻOB prepared their fighters to resist again. The 30,000 remaining Jews who had gone into hiding had established fortified positions. But there was no escape: they would fight until they were either killed or they surrendered.

When the German police and SS auxiliary forces marched into the ghetto on the morning of 19 April under the command of Sammern-Frankenegg, the streets were empty. They ordered the Jews to come out into the roads, shouting and blowing whistles. As the soldiers moved through the streets knocking on doors, cursing and screaming obscenities, they were suddenly ambushed by resistance fighters firing and tossing Molotov cocktails and hand grenades from top floor windows, sewers and alleyways.

Some 750 Jewish fighters were armed with an assortment of arms and ammunition. They were facing two battalions of Waffen-SS, a hundred regular soldiers, and several units of Order Police and Security Police. For the rest of the day the Jewish resistance fighters launched a series of attacks and the Germans sustained fifty-nine casualties. During the afternoon, as fighting intensified, two boys climbed onto the roof of a building in Muranowski Square and raised two flags, the red-and-white Polish flag and the blue-and-white banner of the ŻZW. The square saw some of the most intense fighting of the uprising.

The resistance fighters were sustaining losses and were held down under constant machine gun and mortar fire, but they defended well and it soon became apparent that Sammern-Frankenegg was struggling. Himmler ordered that he be relieved of his command.

On 20 April he was replaced by the ruthless and efficient SS-Brigadeführer Jürgen Stroop. In Stroop's report made after the uprising, he noted:

I myself arrived in Warsaw on 17 April 1943, and took over command of the Grossaktion at 8 o'clock, after the Aktion itself had started at 6 o'clock on the same day... The number of Jews brought out from the houses and held during the first few days was relatively small. It proved that the Jews were hiding in the sewer canals and in specially constructed bunkers. Where it had been assumed during the first days that there were only isolated bunkers, it proved in the course of the Grossaktion that the whole ghetto had been systematically provided with cellars, bunkers and passageways. The passages and bunkers all had access to the sewers. This enabled the Jews to move underground without interference. The Jews also used this network of sewers to escape underground into the Aryan part of the city of Warsaw. There were constant reports that Jews were attempting to escape through the sewer holes … How far the Jews' precautions had gone was demonstrated by many instances of bunkers skilfully laid out with accommodation for entire families, facilities for washing and bathing, toilets, storage bins for arms and ammunition.

There were different bunkers for poor and for rich Jews. It was extremely difficult for the task force to discover the individual bunkers owing to camouflage, and in many cases it was made possible only through betrayal on the part of the Jews. After a few days it was already clear that the Jews would under no circumstances consider voluntary resettlement, but were determined to fight back by every means and with the weapons in their possession. Under Polish Bolshevik leadership so-called fighting units were formed which were armed and paid any price asked for available arms … While at first it had been possible to capture the Jews, who are ordinarily cowards, in considerable numbers, the apprehending of the bandits and Jews became increasingly difficult in the second half of the Grossaktion. Again and again, fighting units of 20 to 30 or more Jewish youths, 18 to 25 years old, accompanied by corresponding numbers of females, renewed the resistance. These fighting units were under orders to continue armed resistance to the end and, if necessary, to escape capture by suicide. One such fighting unit succeeded in climbing out of the sewer through a manhole in so-called Prosta [Street] and to get onto a truck and escape with it (about 30 to 35 bandits). During the armed resistance, females belonging to the fighting units were armed in the same way as the men; some were members of the He-Halutz Movement. It was no rarity for these females to fire pistols with both hands. It happened again and again that they kept pistols and hand-grenades (Polish 'egg' grenades) hidden in their bloomers up to the last moment, to use them against the men of the Waffen-SS, Police and Wehrmacht.

On 19 April a progress report of the uprising was issued from the SS and Police Leader in the Warsaw District to the SS and Police Leader East, Krakow.

Closing of ghetto commenced at 03.00hrs. At 06.00hrs the Waffen-SS was ordered to comb out the remainder of the ghetto at a strength of 16/850.

As soon as the units had entered, strong concerted fire was directed at them by the Jews and bandits. The tank employed in this operation and the two SPW [heavy armoured cars] were attacked with Molotov cocktails. The tank was twice set on fire. This attack with fire by the enemy caused the units employed to withdraw in the first stage. Losses in the first attack were 12 men (6 SS men, 6 Trawniki men). About 08.00hrs the units were sent in again under the command of the undersigned. Although there was again a counterattack, in lesser strength, this operation made it possible to comb out the blocks of buildings according to plan. We succeeded in causing the enemy to withdraw from the roofs and prepared elevated positions into the cellars, bunkers and sewers. Only about 200 Jews were caught during the combing-out operation. Immediately afterwards shock-troop units were directed to known bunkers with orders to pull out the occupants and destroy the bunkers. About 380 Jews were caught in this operation. It was discovered that the Jews were in the sewers. The sewers were completely flooded, to make it impossible to remain there. About 17.30 hrs very strong resistance was met with from one block of buildings, including machine-gun fire. A special battle unit overcame the enemy, and penetrated into the buildings, but without capturing the enemy himself. The Jews and criminals resisted from base to base, and escaped at the last moment through garrets or subterranean passages. About 20.30 hrs the external closure of the ghetto was reinforced.

Over the followed days Stroop's men fought fierce battles with the resistance fighters. Men and women had dug in and were scattered in various buildings. Crude obstacles were erected and defenders were stationed in them armed with their rifles and Molotov cocktails. Fighting occasionally spread outside the ghetto walls. SS-Untersturmführer Hans Dehmke was killed when gunfire detonated a hand grenade he was holding.

To end the uprising and save further embarrassment, Stroop gave the defenders an ultimatum – it was rejected and he ordered his units to burn every house block by block using flamethrowers and artillery, included basements and sewers.

Stroop wrote in his diary:

The resistance offered by the Jews and bandits could be broken only by the energetic, tireless deployment of storm-patrols night and day. On 23 April 1943, the Reichsführer SS, through the Higher SS and Police Führer for the East, in Krakow, issued the order that the Warsaw ghetto be combed out with maximum severity and ruthless determination. I therefore decided to carry out the total destruction of the Jewish quarter by burning down all residential blocks, including the blocks attached to the armament factories. One by one the factories were systematically cleared and then destroyed by fire. Almost always the Jews then emerged from their hiding places and bunkers. Not rarely, the Jews stayed in the burning houses until the heat and fear of being burned to death caused them to jump from the upper floors after they had thrown mattresses and other upholstered objects from the burning houses to the street. With broken bones they would then try to crawl across the street into buildings which were not yet, or only partially, in flames. Often, too, Jews changed their hiding places during the night, by shifting into the ruins of buildings already burned out and taking refuge there until they were found by one of the shock troop units.

The surviving fighters were compelled to move from their defensive positions. Some left under a hail of fire, others took refuge in the sewers. Some were surrounded and had no escape; they fought until they ran out of ammunition. Stroop's men combed the area for more hideouts using dogs and smoke bombs. Sometimes they flooded suspected hideouts or destroyed them with high explosives.

Some fighters committed suicide. During one patrol, SS soldiers found the dugout in Mila Street which had served as the ŻOB's main command post. Inside they came across the scene of a mass suicide. It was later discovered that they included the commander of the ŻOB, Mordechaj Anielewicz, and his deputy Marek Edelman.

The uprising officially ended on 16 May when the Great Synagogue was blown up.

Those that had been captured, including some women and children, were interrogated. Some 13,000 Jews had been killed in the ghetto during the uprising, half of whom had been burnt or succumbed to smoke inhalation. The rest were deported to Majdanek and Treblinka death camps. The German death toll is uncertain. It is estimated there were some 110 casualties of which 16 were killed. This does not include the Trawniki men and Jewish collaborators. The Germans officially announced that there were few casualties and that the 'insurgents' had incurred huge losses during their 'futile' resistance.

While it was considered something of a disgrace among SS leaders that the Jewish community had dared to rise up, Stroop was determined to make the best of it. Photographs had been taken during the uprising and an official report was later prepared for Himmler by the Chief of the SS and Police in Krakow, Friedrich Kruger. The report recounted the Uprising and its successful suppression. It was titled *Es gibt keinen Jüdischen Wohnbezirk in Warschau mehr!* (*The Jewish Quarter of Warsaw is No More!*) With Stroop's help, Kruger put together three leather-bound copies, one of which was a souvenir album for Himmler. These photographs represent the bulk of the imagery in this chapter.

(**Below**) Having received advance warning of the deportation, the entire population of the ghetto disappeared into prepared hiding places before the Germans arrived. Non-compliance with orders to assemble for deportation was combined with hit and run attacks on German units, which forced their temporary withdrawal. When the first clashes of the uprising began, SS-Brigadeführer Jürgen Stroop was called from Lvov to suppress the rebellion and liquidate the 56,000 remaining Jews. In this photograph SS and police officers look on as Stroop discusses attacks on Niska and Muranowska Streets with Police Adjutant Karl Kaleschke. (*USHMM, Instytut Pamieci Narodowej*)

(**Opposite, above**) Stroop can be seen briefing 'Trawniki' helpers during a clearing operation of the ghetto. Supported by regular SS soldiers, the Trawniki were ordered to round up the remaining Jews and either march them out of the ghetto or load them onto waiting trucks.

(**Opposite, below**) Stroop (second from left) gathers information from a civilian on the second day of the suppression of the uprising. Accompanying him are various officers of his staff: SS-Führer Conrad (left), Kaleschke (partially hidden), SS-Untersturmführer Karl Brandt (third from right), SS-Untersturmführer Schwarz (second from right), and an Untersturmführer in the SD. (*USHMM, Louis Gonda*)

Two photographs showing German policemen operating an Sd.Kfz.2 radio command car during the initial stages of the uprising. The original German caption reads: 'In the radio car of the command post'. (NARA)

Jewish labourers are forced by SS troops to evacuate a Warsaw ghetto factory during the uprising. The original German caption reads: 'Vacating the factories!' (NARA)

A column of Jews being deported from the ghetto to the rail station. They are heading North to Umschlagplatz on Zamenhofa Street near Kupiecka. In the background are buildings of Zamenhofa 30–40 block. (NARA)

(**Above**) Jews captured by the SS march past the St Zofia hospital along Nowolipie Street towards the Umschlagplatz for deportation. (*USHMM, Howard Kaplan*)

(**Opposite, above**) Jews captured by the SS are interrogated by the ghetto wall before being sent to the Umschlagplatz. The original German caption reads: 'Search and Interrogation'. (*NARA*)

(**Opposite, below**) An SS officer questions two Jewish resistance fighters during the suppression of the uprising as Stroop (rear, centre) and his security detail look on. The original German caption reads: 'Jewish traitors'. (*NARA*)

Jewish Rabbis: Lipa Kaplan, Eliyahu Levin, Mendel Alter, Yankel Levin and Herschel Rappaport in front of Nowolipie 32. The original German caption reads: 'Jewish rabbis'. *(NARA)*

Bodies of Jewish policemen executed by the SS. Revenge attacks like this were common across the ghetto. The SS took the view that the police bore the blame for not suspecting an uprising and being unable to control the situation. *(USHMM, Leopold Page Photographic Collection)*

Two photographs showing SS troops arresting the Jewish department heads of the Brauer armaments factory. The original German caption reads: 'The Jewish department heads of the armament firm Brauer'. (*NARA*)

(**Opposite, above**) Officers discussing the evacuation of the factory at Nalewki Street. The guard on the left is Josef Blösche. While the battle continued inside the ghetto, Polish resistance groups also engaged the Germans at various locations outside the ghetto walls, firing at German sentries and positions. (*NARA*)

(**Opposite, below**) SS troops guard members of the Jewish resistance. The original German caption reads: 'Bandits!' (*NARA*)

(**Above**) Soldiers advancing along a street. The damage is evident as the troops comb each street, setting fire to the buildings or throwing smoke grenades through the windows of suspected hideouts. (*NARA*)

(**Opposite**) Two photographs showing damage caused by the Germans. After five days of the uprising the deadline for 'voluntary' evacuation had passed and the Germans recommenced what was known as the 'pacification action' of the area – which involved setting fire to many buildings. Heavy fighting took place as partisans barricaded in houses kept the Germans from advancing into some areas. (*NARA*)

(**Above**) A building razed by the SS. When there were no more places to live, the partisans descended to the underground shelters occupied by the civilian population. (*USHMM, Howard Kaplan*)

(**Opposite**) An apartment building burns. Armed encounters were fought mostly at night; in the daytime the ghetto was usually quiet. (*USHMM, Instytut Pamieci Narodowej*)

(**Above**) SS personal converse while watching a building burn. By the second week of the uprising the situation was becoming more grave for the Jewish Resistance. Food was scarce and so was ammunition. They also had no communication outside the ghetto to the 'Aryan side', and so were unable to receive weapons from the Polish Home Army. (*USHMM, Instytut Pamieci Narodowej*)

(**Opposite, above**) Smoke rises from buildings razed by the SS. The view is from Walicow Street looking south. (*USHMM, Instytut Pamieci Narodowej*)

(**Opposite, below**) Making his way along a street in choking dust and thick smoke, protecting his mouth and nose with a handkerchief, is an SS-Obersturmbannführer. This man would have commanded a battalion-sized unit during the uprising. (*NARA*)

(**Above**) A staff car with a sidecar combination closely following advances along a dust-filled street. (*NARA*)

(**Above & opposite, above**) Two photographs taken at different angles looking north showing a housing block being destroyed in Zamenhofa Street. The other image shows a column of Jewish civilians being escorted along the street to be deported to a labour or death camp. *(NARA)*

(**Opposite, below**) An SS soldier watches as a housing block burns. The original German caption reads: 'Destruction of a housing block'. *(NARA)*

(**Above**) A street devastated by reprisals from the Germans as they marched through, burning and blowing up buildings as they went. (*NARA*)

(**Opposite & following**) This is a series of photographs taken in sequence showing the SS forcing out Jews and insurgents from an apartment block in Niska Street. The first image shows SS soldiers with what appears to be a Jewish family being arrested in front of the building. They have evidently climbed out of a ground floor window. One man, who appears to be an insurgent, raises his arms in surrender. The SS are aware there are more people resisting and hiding inside the building on the upper floors, and set it alight to force them out. The original German caption reads: 'Bandits jump to escape capture. Men preparing to commit suicide by jumping off the upper floors of 23 and 25 Niska Street 22 April 1943'. There were numerous buildings throughout the city where members of the Home Army hid with Jewish families. (*NARA*)

German police and SS personnel arrest Jews on Nowolipie Street. Extensive searches were made throughout the ghetto, and many frightened and bewildered Jews surrendered. *(USHMM, Howard Kaplan)*

Polish fire fighters and SS officers in the Warsaw ghetto during the suppression of the uprising. The original Polish caption reads: 'The Germans set fire to the buildings evacuated by the Jews. From a balcony on the top floor a family of five or six people jumped to their deaths. They didn't leave earlier as ordered and then they couldn't run away. We didn't help them even though technically we could have'. *(USHMM, Howard Kaplan)*

(**Opposite, above**) Stroop was determined to bring about a halt to the uprising and ordered his troops to set buildings alight as they advanced. Often there were sporadic exchanges of fire, or wholesale surrenders of Home Army fighters along with families. (*NARA*)

(**Opposite, below**) An artillery gun gets prepared for action. Heavy guns were used during the uprising to destroy buildings, and to blow up parts of the ghetto wall to allow troops to comb the area more easily and infiltrate potential or known hideouts. (*NARA*)

(**Above**) A burnt-out building after the SS had set it alight to force out anyone attempting to hide. (*NARA*)

The first of five photographs showing a bunker used by the Jewish resistance. The original German caption reads: 'Pictures of so-called residential bunkers'. (NARA)

Jews captured during the uprising are led by the SS to the Umschlagplatz for deportation. The original German caption reads: 'To the Umschlagplatz' or 'Deportation of Jews'. *(NARA)*

A German unit uses an artillery piece to blast part of the ghetto wall and a suspected building hiding resistance fighters inside. The original German caption reads: 'Resistance pocket. Cannon on Zamenhofa Street shooting north at resistance in Gęsia 20 building'. *(NARA)*

A debris-filled street. While the battle escalated inside the ghetto, Polish resistance groups AK and GL engaged German units between 19 and 23 April at six different locations outside the ghetto walls, firing at German sentries and positions. (*USHMM, Instytut Pamieci Narodowej*)

Depicting the extensive damage wrought to the ghetto. Note a huge hole in the ghetto wall that has been blasted by artillery to access parts of the ghetto quickly. (*NARA*)

Two photographs taken in sequence showing a German 10.5cm gun crew shelling a housing block. (*NARA*)

An SS soldier stands among ruins in the Warsaw ghetto. The Jews knew that their uprising was doomed and their survival was unlikely, but they still continued resisting. (*NARA*)

The first of four photographs showing damage to the ghetto. Many of the buildings were gutted by high explosives or by flamethrowers. *(NARA)*

Mattresses and furniture lie piled next to an apartment building to provide a place for the inhabitants to jump during the suppression of the Warsaw ghetto uprising. The original German caption reads: 'A place that had been readied for jumping and escape'. (NARA)

SS troops search ruined buildings for survivors. *(NARA)*

(**Opposite, above**) SS soldiers conferring standing next to part of the ghetto wall that has been partly demolished by artillery. (*NARA*)

(**Above**) A photograph depicting some of the destruction that Stroop's men wrought on the ghetto. Part of the remains of the ghetto wall is visible. (*NARA*)

(**Opposite, below**) A typical street in the ghetto that has been laid to waste by the uprising. After two weeks of fighting every street in the ghetto had been reduced to ruin. Houses were burnt out or partly-standing wrecks. (*NARA*)

SS soldiers pause to eat during the suppression of the Warsaw ghetto uprising. By end of April organized defence had mostly collapsed. Surviving fighters and thousands of remaining Jewish civilians took to hiding in the sewer system, in dugouts or in the ruins of the ghetto, referred to as 'bunkers' by Germans. (*USHMM, Louis Gonda*)

SS troops force Jews to dig out the entrance to a bunker on the twentieth day of the uprising. The original German caption reads: 'A bunker is opened'. (*NARA*)

Commanding officers observing as Home Army fighters are pulled from one of the many dugouts that were concealed in the ruins of the ghetto. The Germans used dogs to search for hideouts, and then often dropped smoke grenades inside to force people out. Sometimes they flooded the hideouts or destroyed them with explosives. On occasion, shootouts occurred. *(NARA)*

An SS Untersturmführer interrogates a Jewish resistance fighter captured on the twenty-first day of the suppression of the Warsaw ghetto uprising. *(USHMM, Louis Gonda)*

Jürgen Stroop and his men standing nearby as Jews emerge from a bunker during the Warsaw ghetto uprising. *(NARA)*

SS troops walk past a block of burning housing. The original German caption reads: 'An assault squad'. (NARA)

Jewish families surrender to the SS. The original German caption reads: 'Smoking out the Jews and bandits'. (NARA)

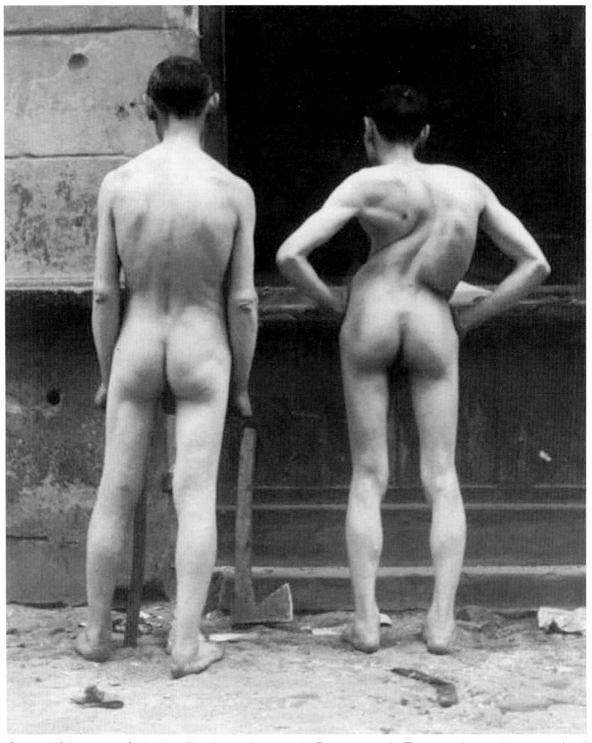

Captured fighters were further humiliated once they were in German custody. They were beaten, interrogated and stripped of their clothes. In the original German caption to this photo it reads: 'Dregs of humanity. All the prisoners were stripped during the search'. (NARA)

Jews captured by the SS are lined up against a wall before being searched for weapons. The original German caption reads: 'Before the search'. *(NARA)*

Captured Jewish civilians in front of 31 and 33 Miła viewed from Zamenhofa Street. These bewildered people were hiding, fearing for their lives. The Germans often treated hiding civilians as resistance fighters. The original German caption reads: 'They were also found in the underground bunkers'. *(NARA)*

(**Above**) Hehalutz women captured with weapons. These women were all deported to Majdanek death camp. The person on the right of the photograph is Małka Zdrojewicz. She survived the camp; the other two were killed. (*NARA*)

(**Opposite**) Two photographs taken in sequence showing SS assault troops that have captured two Jewish resistance fighters after pulling them from a bunker. The original German caption reads alternately: 'Pulled from a bunker' or 'Bandits'. (*NARA*)

(**Opposite, above**) What appear to be captured civilians are forced by their captors to lie face down in the rubble from a bunker between Nowolipie and Smocza streets. The fear of the two females left of the picture can clearly be seen. (*NARA*)

(**Above**) Civilians and fighters have been captured and forced to lie head down in the rubble. All have been executed. The original German caption reads: 'Bandits destroyed in battle. Executed Jews'.

(**Opposite, below**) Jews captured during the Warsaw ghetto uprising are marched to the Umschlagplatz for deportation. (*NARA*)

(**Opposite, above**) Jews captured by the SS during the suppression of the Warsaw ghetto uprising board a truck bound for either a labour or death camp. (*USHMM, Instytut Pamieci Narodowej*)

(**Opposite, below**) Aerial view of a column of German troops marching down Sienna Street shortly after the destruction of the Warsaw ghetto. (*USHMM, Tad Brezkis*)

(**Above**) Clandestine photograph of the destroyed Warsaw ghetto in the summer of 1943. Tad Brezkis was a Polish photographer. Having witnessed the destruction of the Warsaw ghetto, he returned a few months later to take almost forty clandestine pictures of the destroyed ghetto with a Leica camera. (*USHMM, Tad Brezkis*)

Chapter Three

The Polish Home Army Uprising 1944

After the 1943 uprising the SS and police blew up the houses in the ghetto and razed the streets to a rubble ruin. Slave labourers were then brought in and a concentration camp was erected. The camp was operational by July 1943, and although regarded by the Germans as a minor camp for labour and transit, 4,500 people still died there.

In some areas small resistance groups had got together again. However, this time the Germans were quick to react, and the Warsaw Security Service (SD) under Dr Ludwig Hahn, and men of the 3rd Battalion of the 23rd SS Police Regiment commanded by SS-Sturmbannführer Otton Bundtke, undertook a number of arrests and executions.

But a few small groups still managed to escape the ghetto and joined the Polish Home Army in Warsaw's main city.

In June 1944 news reached Warsaw and the Home Army that the Allies had landed in northern France. A few weeks later the Red Army mobilised their summer offensive.

As the Russians came close to Warsaw, Home Army leaders began making plans for resistance in the capital. They intended to rise up against the Germans, seize the city, or large parts of it, and retain it long enough for the Red Army to march into the capital. The Home Army were aware that any armed resistance would be met with a brutal response by the SS. For this reason it was intended that the rising would be timed to coincide with a Russian assault into the city. Then the SS would be overwhelmed and unable to respond efficiently. Yet, unknown to the Home Army, the Soviets had no such plans. Their objective was to hold their bridgeheads and sit tight.

In late July some Russian units did undertake a series of probing attacks towards Warsaw, and news reached Home Army intelligence that the Red Army had launched a general assault on the capital. This was what the Home Army had long been waiting for and its leaders quickly responded. Their plan was to prevent the

Germans bringing up reserves and cut off their supply lines. The Germans would be pushed back across the Vistula under Soviet pressure, and then troops in great numbers would enter the city which would become a battlefield between the Germans and Russians. It was agreed that the time was right for attack, in spite of limited intelligence on the Soviet advance.

On the morning of 1 August, orders were sent out to prepare for attack. A number of command posts never received the instruction, and there was a serious shortage of ammunition and weapons. Much of the arms caches had been removed from Warsaw in preparation for an uprising in the countryside. Nevertheless, hundreds of Home Army fighters made their way to their assembly points as inconspicuously as possible.

The Home Army command structure was divided into eight city districts. Its military formations consisted of battalions, companies, and platoons. Company of 50–100 men were usually named after their commanding officer. On 1 August over 600 companies fanned out across the city, each with a specific street or building to defend. No warning was given to the civilian population that were still moving about the city, as absolute secrecy was required.

At 5.00pm, as planned, the attack was launched. The main German strongpoints were targeted first by groups of Home Army fighters wearing their distinctive red and white arm bands. Shooting was heavy and in the crossfire civilians were wounded or killed. A number of Home Army fighters charged the Prudential Building killing German soldiers as they made their way to the roof to hoist the Home Army flag. A German ammunition and arms warehouse was captured along with the main post office, the railway depot in Praga, and the power station.

Fighting in the city was fierce with buildings set on fire by hand grenades and Molotov cocktails. A number of streets were heavily fortified and some buildings barricaded with well-armed Home Army fighters. Losses were high and within a few hours some 2,500 fighters of the Home Army had been killed. In fact, the losses were similar to those of Allied soldiers on the Normandy beaches on D-Day. However, they did not deter the Home Army, and all over the city they continued fighting.

Nazi reaction was swift. Himmler ordered a special corps to be rushed to Warsaw. The commander was SS-Obergruppenführer Erich von dem Bach-Zelewski. Under him were 17,000 men of the 'pacification' troop named 'Korpsgruppe Bach'. Assisting the brigade was SS-Gruppenführer Heinz Reinefarth, in charge of Kampfgruppe Reinefarth, a 'pacification' unit consisting of two battalions of SS-Oberführer Oskar Dirlewanger's SS soldiers and the 11th Azerbaijani Regiment including several other Ordnungspolizei and SS rear area units. These consisted of the SS RONA Brigade from the Russian National Liberation Army under Brigadeführer Kaminski, 572nd and 580th Cossack Battalions, 608th Special Defence Battalion, a Posnanian militarized police battalion, a Luftwaffe guard regiment, and a reserve battalion of the Hermann Göring Panzer-Fallschirmjäger which was operating east of Warsaw.

On 5 August units of Korpsgruppe Bach were put into action. First they entered the western suburbs where they caught hundreds of civilians hiding in their houses and slaughtered them. No one was spared, not even children, babies, nuns, nurses, hospital patients and doctors. It is estimated that 40,000 civilians were killed in the Wola area alone. Initially German policy was designed to crush the Poles' will to fight and put the uprising to a quick end. But Warsaw did erupt in heavy fighting. The next day Bach-Zelewski ordered that only men were to be killed. Other civilians were to be taken to a transit camp outside the city.

Elsewhere fighting with the 'rebels' continued. Korpsgruppe Bach set up fire points and road blocks and then fought its way along the main streets using armour to shield the infantry. As the tanks moved up, Home Army fighters in their hideouts often let them come, then the soldiers moved and the fighters began to fire. Tanks were used to destroy whole buildings at close range. However, Home Army fighters with grenades and anti-tank rifles were sometimes able to cripple the tanks in the narrow streets. In fact, it was on 3 August that the Home Army captured their first panzer. They then repaired it and drove it into action against their former owners.

After the first week of the uprising some parts of Warsaw consisted of rubble and half-shattered and burning buildings. Other large parts remained totally intact and Home Army fighters had taken control of much of the capital. However, they had not driven out the Germans, and there was no communication on developments east of the Vistula. It appeared that the Red Army assault on Warsaw had not materialised. This may have been because the Soviets could not advance into the capital as it had run into determined German resistance, or it may have been a deliberate decision of the Soviets to let the Poles do the fighting for them. It should be noted that when some Home Army detachments met with Soviet officers outside Warsaw, they were disarmed, their commanders shot, and the men forcibly recruited into the Red Army. Either way the Home Army was compelled to fight on its own.

The Home Army fighters had by this time stabilized their positions in the Old Town, the city centre, and the southern suburbs. They still proved very capable fighters and seemed to be getting stronger despite heavy bombardments on their positions. They repeatedly reoccupied strongpoints that were lost and reinforced barricades. Much of their success was due to their improvisation. Initially they possessed only one gun for every two men, but this ratio was improving thanks to a network of underground factories and repair shops which ensured the frequent supply of basic armaments. Home Army fighters also armed themselves with German MP40s, Karbiner 98K bolt action rifles, and even STG44 machine guns, captured from enemy stores. Some also took to wearing captured German SS camouflage smocks, German steel helmets or M43 field caps. In the thick of battle, the only way to distinguish friend from their foe was by the Home Army armband, or a red and white stripe painted crudely around the SS helmet.

Over the next weeks a stalemate of sorts reigned in Warsaw, with the Germans trying to pacify the uprising and preventing the Home Army fighters interfering with front line operations. The Home Army's priority was to retain their strongpoints and keep going as long as possible until relief arrived. Sappers were a constant concern for the Germans. The famous 'minerki' female sappers often picked off soldiers at will and placed booby traps in buildings.

By the end of August, Bach's hard-pressed men were still struggling to control the city. They were alarmed that the rising was going to continue into September and seriously obstruct plans to turn Warsaw into a front-line German fortress.

However Polish losses were intolerable and it was considered there should be a capitulation agreement. The Germans too were willing to contemplate concessions to bring about a halt to hostilities. However, they would not agree to any settlement unless the entire population were first removed from the city. The Home Army required guaranteed safe passage. Fighting continued for another week until proper negotiations started. Over the period of 8–10 September German representatives and the Polish Red Cross agreed on removing 20,000–25,000 civilians. Most were women, children, and the elderly and they were marched west out the city. With the evacuations underway, the Germans called for a general capitulation. They also outlined conceding 'combatant rights' and promising 'no reprisals'. However, with the lack of trust, there was no agreement, and fighting continued in spite of both sides still wanting an end to hostilities.

For the next weeks in September fierce battles raged day by day. Slowly the defenders were being ground down and driven into small blocks of barricaded streets.

On 26 September there was a two-hour truce allowing 9,000 civilians to be evacuated from the Mokotov district. A number of Home Army fighters, fearing artillery shelling and aerial bombardments, moved into the sewers.

Finally the Home Army commander, General Bor-Komorowski, applied for permission to surrender his forces. Only the city centre was still holding out. A capitulation order of the remaining Polish forces was signed on 2 October. All fighting ceased that evening. According to the terms of the surrender, the Germans promised to treat Home Army soldiers in accordance with the Geneva Convention and treat the civilian population humanely. The next day, the Germans began to disarm the Home Army soldiers.

(**Left**) A portrait image of SS-Obergruppenführer Erich von dem Bach-Zelewski. Bach-Zelewski was an experienced anti-partisan commander in charge of warfare against those deemed enemies of the state. His barbaric methods produced a high civilian death toll with his units combing villages and towns and slaughtering them in their hundreds. His anti-partisan control did not produce very good results, but he excelled by indiscriminately murdering innocent people and inflating the figures of enemy losses. His units accomplished little more than temporarily forcing out partisans. On 2 August 1944 he was given command of all German troops in Warsaw and ordered to suppress the uprising. Zelewski was not a good military commander and did not want his troops to be drawn into a protracted urban battle. His plan was to crush the Poles' will to fight as quickly as possible. Warsaw resisted for two months during which Zelewski's units murdered 200,000 civilians and destroyed much of the city.

(**Right**) A photo of Waffen-SS Brigadeführer Bronislav Vladislavovich Kaminski after his capture in 1945. Kaminski was a Russian anti-communist collaborationist and became commander of the Lokot Republic and built an anti-partisan formation made up of people from the so-called Lokot territory. His new brigade reinforced with volunteers drafted from Soviet PoWs at nearby Nazi concentration camps, was primarily used to fight guerrillas as well as to carry on a propaganda campaign against Jewish Bolshevism and Soviet partisans. By March 1944, the brigade was renamed Volksheer-Brigade Kaminski and within weeks attached to SS-Kampfgruppe von Gottberg, which also included the notorious Dirlewanger unit, and participated in mass murder and security operations. The brigade was later absorbed as a part of the Waffen-SS and renamed Waffen-Sturm-Brigade RONA (Russian National Liberation Army – Russkaya Osvoboditelnaya Narodnaya Armiya). In August 1944, Kaminski leading his notorious group of soldiers was sent to Warsaw to assist in suppressing the uprising. On 18 August Kaminski was killed.

(**Opposite, above left**) A portrait photo of SS-Oberführer Oskar Dirlewanger. Dirlewanger was a sadist described as the most evil man in the SS. He had experience of anti-partisan operations. He was not averse to pacifying areas by herding civilians into barns and setting them alight. He would also march villagers over minefields. He was the ideal candidate to lead his newly built 'storm brigade' to assist in the suppression of the Warsaw Uprising. His Brigade of 2,500 contained 1,900 convicted criminals, including many classed as criminally insane. The Polish resistance inflicted heavy casualties on them.

(**Opposite, above right**) A portrait photograph of the scar-faced SS-Gruppenführer Heinz Reinefarth. Before the Warsaw Uprising Reinefarth had been assigned the job of SS and Police leader in Reichsgau Wartheland (the Polish Poznan Voivodeship annexed by Germany in 1939). In this post he was responsible for organising repressions against Poles and other nationalities. As a commander, Reinefarth was callous and barbaric, and had got results from his methods. He was ordered to organise a military unit consisting of personnel from various security units and move to Warsaw in early August 1944. On arrival his forces, now renamed Kampfgruppe Reinefarth, were included in Korpsgruppe Bach and given instructions to quell the rebellion. For his actions during the Warsaw uprising oak leaves were added to his Knight's Cross.

(**Opposite, below**) A group photograph showing the Polish Home Army (Armia Krajowa, AK). This was the dominant Polish resistance movement in Poland, occupied Nazi Germany and Russia. It was formed in February 1942 from the Zwiazek Walki Zbrinej (Armed Resistance). Over the next two years it absorbed most other Polish underground forces. Its allegiance was to the Polish government in exile and it constituted the armed wing of what became known as the ' Polish Underground State'. (*USHMM, George Gerzon (Gerzon Trzcina)*)

(**Above**) Heinz Reinefarth (middle of photo) at his command post in Warsaw in August 1944. In two days from 5 August the units of Reinefarth and Dirlewanger murdered tens of thousands of civilians in the 'Wola Massacre'.

In Wolska Street, Heinz Reinefarth, pictured left in Cossack headgear, with Jakub Bondarenko, commander of the Kuban Cossack 5th Infantry regiment.

Waffen-SS troops can be seen marching into Warsaw in early August 1944. Some 17,000 troops would become embroiled in heavy fighting against the Polish Home Army.

Officers from what was known as the Hermann Göring Korps in Poland in the summer of 1944. The officers are attending what appears to be a demonstration of the new division. The division left Italy in July 1944 and was transferred for defensive action near Warsaw. It fought in front of Warsaw alongside SS-Panzer Divisions Totenkopf and Wiking, and the 4th and 19th Panzer Divisions. Their actions would end up decimating two of the Soviet armies east and south-east of Warsaw and delaying the Russian advance into Warsaw.

Hermann Göring unit commanders and staff officers receive their orders. Behind them on the dirt track is a 7.5cm Sturmgeschütz III. On 1 August counter-attacks launched by the 19th Panzer Division and Hermann Göring units managed to penetrate 2nd Tank Army's defensive front. On 2 August the 4th Panzer Division joined the battle, stemming further Russian assaults towards Warsaw.

Two photographs showing officers of the Hermann Göring Korps attending a demonstration of the new division. The Korps formed part of the defensive measures along the Vistula in summer 1944 and assisted in the defence in front of Warsaw.

Panzerkorps Hermann Göring grenadiers listen to their company commander from the engine deck of an assault gun before going into action near Warsaw. In spite of the strength of the German defensive effort, by late July the 8th Guards Tank Corps had closed to within 15 miles of Warsaw's eastern suburb of Praga. As a consequence, German forces including the Göring Panzerkorps fought hard to prevent them entering the city. The Polish Home Army inside Warsaw thought the Russians would soon enter the capital and ordered the uprising to commence.

Commanding officers of the SS Sturmbrigade RONA conferring with an aid of a map of Warsaw. In the centre is Major Ivan Denisovich. The unit committed numerous atrocities during the uprising. However, the SS leadership found the brigade too undisciplined and unreliable, and as a result German commanders removed it from Warsaw. In late August it was sent to Slovakia and deployed against Slovak partisans.

(**Above**) A typical defensive position erected by the Polish Home Army in Warsaw. Here the fighters have used rubble from a building as a barricade. Although the position was a crude form of defence, the Home Army fighters were able to defend and attack from these rubble barricades, often holding back the enemy with some success. (*Bender*)

(**Opposite, above**) A Hetzer tank destroyer abandoned on Napoleon Square after evidently coming up against stiff resistance. Note the crude barricade erected across the street, which was effective enough to halt this vehicle.

(**Opposite, below**) This photograph was taken on 3 August. It shows a group of resistance fighters from 'Chrobry I' Battalion in front of German police station 'Nordwache' at the junction of Chłodna and Żelazna Street. (*Bender*)

A member of the Zoska battalion of the Home Army escorts two of the 348 Jews liberated from the Gęsiówka concentration camp by the battalion during the 1944 Warsaw Uprising. Most of these survivors joined the Zośka unit and fought in the Warsaw uprising. (USHMM)

Prisoners of the Gęsiówka concentration camp and the Zośka fighters following the liberation of the camp in August 1944. (Bender)

This photograph was taken on 5 August in Gęsiówka. The Home Army fighters are dressed in stolen German uniforms and are armed with German weapons. From left: Wojciech Omyła 'Wojtek', Juliusz Bogdan Deczkowski 'Laudański' and Tadeusz Milewski 'Ćwik'. Milewski was killed on that day. Omyła was killed on two days later on 8 August. *(USHHM, Juliusz Bogdan Deczkowski)*

(**Opposite**) Two photographs of a captured German Panther tank which has been turned against its former owners. This vehicle was part of the armoured Wacek platoon of Battalion Zośka under command of Waclaw Micuta. It was used by the battalion during its capture of the Gęsiówka concentration camp. (*USHMM, Juliusz Bogdan Deczkowski*)

(**Above, left**) A machine gun crew during a break east of Warsaw. These soldiers formed part of the Warsaw garrison and comprised some 11,000 troops under General Rainer Stahel. During the uprising Stahel was replaced as overall commander by Bach-Zelewski in early August. As the fighting inside Warsaw intensified troops were withdrawn from defensive action east of Warsaw to join the newly-formed Korpsgruppe-Bach.

(**Above, right**) Waffen-SS troops rest in the rubble during a lull in the fighting. Korpsgruppe Bach comprised of some 17,000 men by mid-August. They were divided into two Kampfgruppe, the first under General Rohr, which included 1,700 soldiers of the anti-communist SS Sturmbrigade RONA, also known as the Kaminski Brigade made up of Russian, Belorussian and Ukrainian collaborators. The other Kampfgruppe, under Heinz Reinefarth, consisted of Attack Group Dirlewanger, the Aserbaidschanische Legion, part of the Ostlegionen troop, Attack Group Reck, Attack Group Schmidt and various support and backup units. The force also included some 5,000 regular troops, 4,000 Luftwaffe personnel, anti-aircraft artillery posts, about 2,000 soldiers from Sentry Regiment Warsaw (Wacht-regiment Warschau), four infantry battalions (Patz, Baltz, Nos 996 and 997), and an SS reconnaissance squadron.

German troops east of Warsaw during a pause in the fighting, evidently playing some type of game. During the uprising there were German units stationed in and around Warsaw with police and SS and ad hoc auxiliary units, including detachments of the Bahnschütz (rail guard), Werkschütz (factory guard), units of Polish Volksdeutsche (ethnic Germans in Poland) and Soviet former PoWs of the Sonderdienst and Sonderabteilung paramilitary units.

This photograph was taken on the River Vistula showing the Kierbedź Bridge viewed from the Praga district of Warsaw towards Royal Castle and the Old Town. Note the smoke rising into the air. The Home Army fighters' plan was to capture the bridges across the Vistula to make contact with Russian forces. This was never achieved.

A Home Army fighter can be seen negotiating the rubble. Behind him sit knocked-out Sturmgeschütz III assault guns. During the war the StuG III proved its worth, especially in clearing urban areas. However, it was limited by its fixed turret and as a result many were lost. *(Bender)*

A blurred action photo showing a number of Panther tanks operating slowly in the city. Tanks were vulnerable in urbanized fighting, and as a result they were often either knocked out of action or the crews abandoned them, leaving the vehicles to fall into the hands of the Polish Home Army. *(Bender)*

(**Above**) Two photographs showing the Goliath tracked mine or Leichter Ladungsträger Goliath (Goliath Light Charge Carrier Sd.Kfz.302). This unmanned disposable ground demolition vehicle was primarily used for destroying tanks, disrupting dense infantry formations, and demolition of buildings and bridges.

(**Opposite, above**) A heavy MG42 machine gun crew with their weapon attached to a Lafette 34 sustained-fire mount. The MG42 proved its capabilities in both offensive and defensive actions. Its dependability was second to none and every unit of the Waffen-SS and German army was equipped with this weapon.

(**Opposite, below**) In a typical defensive position is a heavy MG42 machine gunner with his weapon attached to the Lafette 34 sustained fire mount. To the gunner's right are two soldiers, one armed with the MP40 9mm Maschinenpistole, the other with the MP34 Maschinenpistole. MP34s were used by Waffen-SS units in the early stages of the war. It was then allocated to line-of-communications and reserve units, including military police and Feldgendarmerie detachments. This weapon was more than likely used by police units in Warsaw and used by this soldier in the uprising.

A German grenadier prepares to fire at an enemy target with a Karbiner 98K bolt action rifle, which was the standard infantryman's weapon during the war. Attached to his belt he wears ammunition pouches and a canteen bottle. During the uprising the weather was hot and humid. This coupled with the dust and smoke meant that soldiers were constantly in need of water.

As the fighting intensified, greater German firepower was required. In this photograph the crew of a Sturmpanzer 43 Brummbar armoured infantry support gun can be seen operating in Warsaw. This vehicle was part of Sturmpanzer-Kompanie z.b.v. 218, which was raised in August 1944. It was sent to Warsaw where it was attached to Panzer Abteilung (Fkl) 302.

Heavy German bombardments start fires at an intersection at Nowy Šwiat and Warecka Streets. The main objective for the German forces was to set fire to every building and force out all the Home Army fighters.

Waffen-SS troops advance through Warsaw's rubble. A tricycle has been pressed into service to carry supplies for the soldiers such as ammunition boxes, rifles and other gear.

(**Above**) Members of the Home Army wearing a motley collection of captured German uniforms have a well-earned break during a pause in the fighting. (*Bender*)

(**Opposite**) Two photographs taken in sequence showing a German PaK35/36 anti-tank crew manhandling their weapon through the city. This was the standard German anti-tank gun at the outbreak of war. It was small, rugged, well-engineered and reliable. The gun was of conventional type and carried on a two-wheel split-rail carriage of tubular construction with a bolted-on sloped armour shield. Although this gun was out-of-date by this period of the war, in Warsaw it was effective against lighter enemy vehicles and defensive positions.

Two photographs showing a Panther Ausf.G during the uprising. These Panthers, belonging to the 19th Panzer Division, had been withdrawn from the defensive action in front of Warsaw and used for operations inside the city.

A German armoured attack by two Sturmgeschütz III on *Stare Miasto* in the old town of the city.

The first of five photographs taken in sequence showing a column of Panthers from the 1st Panzer Regiment 27 of the 19th Panzer Division on its way towards Warsaw. The division was almost destroyed in early 1944 and was sent to the Netherlands in May 1944 to be refitted. Following the Russian summer offensive, which almost destroyed German Army Group Centre, the division was sent by rail from the Netherlands back to the Eastern Front. It took part in the defence of Warsaw and assisted operations during the uprising for a time.

This photograph, taken on 2 September, shows the young Home Army fighters of what was known as the 'Radosław Group' – soldiers of the Gray Ranks. Gray Ranks was the codename for the underground paramilitary Polish Scouting Association. These fighters had just marched several hours through the Warsaw sewers to evade capture.

Three photographs showing the German self-propelled 60cm bunker-busting Mörser Karl. This monster gun fired a 2,170kg shell up to 6 miles. It had to be accompanied by a crane, a two-piece heavy transport set of railcars, and a number of modified tanks to carry the shells. On 14 August, the Kommando für Sonder-Geräte formed the Army Artillery Battery (Static) 638 Heeres-Artillerie Batterie (bodenständige) with 60cm Karl-Gerät Nr. VI 'Ziu' and was ordered to Warsaw to assist in suppressing the resistance. It arrived at the Warsaw West railway station in the morning of 17 August. The ammunition train arrived the following morning. 'Ziu' was positioned in the Sowiński Park near the statue of General Jozef Sowinski in the Wola district. Though the shells could be deadly, they often did not explode when they hit buildings or soft ground in the city.

(**Above**) The Art Deco style British Prudential Insurance Company building, on Swietokrzyska Street, has received a hit from a 60cm shell from the Mörser Karl Gerät. During the uprising some 1,000 shells, including a single hit by the 2-ton Karl-Gerät mortar shell, badly damaged the building, leaving only the steel framework. However, the building survived the war. This picture was taken by the Polish soldier Sylwester Braun 'Kris' on 28 August.

(**Opposite, above**) German soldiers advance across Theatre Square in Warsaw during operations in September. By this time the Polish Army were slowly being driven from one defensive position to another, often fighting to the death.

(**Opposite, below**) On 27 September this Home Army soldier from the Mokotów District surrenders to German troops. He had evidently been hiding in the sewers.

(**Above**) Female fighters chat and share a cigarette with a wounded comrade in Werecka Street, north Šródmieście district. Pictured is Maria Stypulkowska-Chojecka 'Kama' (centre) and Krzyszof Palester 'Krzych' (right). They are from Battalion Parasol which was a scout battalion of the Home Army. The battalion distinguished itself in numerous underground operations and fought well in the uprising. Note the battalion parasol on the soldiers cap. (*Bender*)

(**Opposite, above**) One method of forcing resistance fighters out of buildings was the flamethrower. This photograph taken in September shows a soldier using a flamethrower, randomly setting fire to any area that might be a hiding place.

(**Opposite, below**) Soldiers advancing along a decimated Focha Street. Gradually the 'rebels' were reduced to fighting in very small areas of the city.

A photograph showing Warsaw civilians from the Wola district being evacuated from the city. On 26 September there was a two-hour truce allowing 9,000 civilians to be evacuated from the Mokotov district.

Chapter Four

Aftermath

The exact losses sustained in the Home Army uprising are unknown and estimates vary. German losses were based on figures of Bach-Zelewski. It is generally agreed that 11,000 Germans were killed or wounded in action. As for the Polish Home Army, around 22,000 were killed or wounded in action. The civilian population suffered far more, with 150,000–200,000 killed. Some 500,000 civilians were forced to surrender into Nazi captivity following the surrender of Warsaw.

The evacuation of the city began on 3 October 1944 with 15,000 Home Army soldiers marching to prearranged entry points to the German lines. Most were still wearing red-and-white armbands and carrying weapons – anything from captured Panzerfaust to Sten guns, revolvers and rifles. When they reached German lines at Filter Street, Napoleon Square or Vola Street, they deposited their arms.

As the military evacuation was nearing completion, streams of civilians came pouring along the roads heading towards Durchgangslager 121 transit camp in Pruszkow. Many were dirty, exhausted, starving, sick and wounded, but were compelled to walk the 10 miles to their destination. The Germans appeared to be keeping to their word, and there was initially no retribution.

As for the Home Army, most were sent, as agreed, to regular PoW camps run by the Wehrmacht.

After the evacuation large parts of the city were demolished. According to German plans, 'Warsaw was to be turned into nothing more than a military transit station'. Over a period of three months demolition squads used flamethrowers and explosives to obliterate every building, special attention being made to demolish historical monuments.

By January 1945 almost all of the buildings had been razed to the ground. It is estimated that 10,500 buildings, 900 historical buildings, 145 schools, 14 libraries, 25 churches, and most of the city's historical monuments had been destroyed. A million inhabitants lost all of their possessions.

As for the civilians that had been sent to transit camps, some 100,000, in contravention of the evacuation agreement, were sent to Germany as slave labourers, and several thousand were sent to concentration camps such as Mauthausen, Ravensbrück and Auschwitz.

On the front line east of Warsaw, the Red Army had been holding its positions and building up its forces. It had for weeks been fighting to the south of the city to seize bridgeheads over the Vistula, and to the north for bridgeheads over the Narew.

Finally, on 12 January 1945, the Soviet winter offensive was launched against the weakening German front in Poland. 'Fortress Warsaw' became encircled and German Army Group A's headquarters issued orders for the city to be abandoned, much to the fury of Hitler. On 17 January Poland's capital fell, or what was left of it; as far as the eye could see there was nothing but rubble and half-shattered buildings.

Had the Russians come to the assistance of the Home Army, then its fate may have been completely different. Stalin probably stood aside to allow the Germans to defeat the Poles because the removal of the anti-communist Polish underground was beneficial to his plans for Poland as a Soviet satellite after the war.

General Bor-Komorowski shakes hands with Bach-Zelewski following the surrender of the Polish Home Army. An official message had been sent to his people stating, 'Warsaw has fallen after having exhausted all means of fighting and all food supplies on the 63rd day of her heroic struggle against the overwhelming superiority of the enemy.' A capitulation order of the remaining Polish forces was signed on 2 October. All fighting ceased that evening. According to the terms of the surrender, the Germans promised to treat Home Army soldiers in accordance with the Geneva Convention and to treat the civilian population humanely. The next day, the Germans began to disarm the Home Army soldiers.

Following the official surrender of the Polish Home Army General Bor-Komorowski can be seen standing in a doorway with Bach-Zelewski flanked by two sentries either side. A German officer appears to be about to salute Bor-Komorowski.

A clandestine photograph of civilian women and children from Warsaw transported to Ravensbrück after the collapse of the Warsaw Uprising. *(USHMM, Anna Hassa Jarosky and Peter Hassa)*

This photograph was taken in October 1944 and shows one of several clandestine images of civilian women and children from Warsaw taken either before or after their arrival in Ravensbrück concentration camp after the collapse of the Warsaw uprising. In contravention to the terms of the surrender, where the Germans had initially promised to treat Home Army soldiers in accordance with the Geneva Convention and to treat the civilian population humanely, some 100,000 civilians were sent to concentration and labour camps. The first phase of these deportations started in October 1944. (*USHMM, Anna Hassa Jarosky and Peter Hassa*)

Warsaw in ruins. Following the uprising, over a period of three months German demolition squads were brought into the city where they were instructed to use flamethrowers and explosives to obliterate every building. Special attention was given to demolishing historical monuments. By January 1945 almost all of the buildings had been razed to the ground. *(USHMM, Israel Gutman)*

Appendix

List of Army Units 1943

German Army units Warsaw August/September 1944

(unit strength in brackets)

Wehrmacht

Oberfeldkommandantur 225, Kommandantur Warschau - Generalleutnant Rainer Stahel

Ostpreussen Grenadier-Regiment 4 (894)

Wachregiment 'Warschau' (400) –
Oberst Lange

Alarmregiment 'Warschau' (400)

Landesschützen Bataillon 996 (650)

Landesschützen Bataillon 997 (650)

Landesschützen Bataillon 998 (650)

Armee-Panzerjäger-Abteilung 743 (120),
28 × Jagdpanzer 38

Panzer-Zerstörer-Bataillon 743, ett kompani

Pionier-Bataillon 654 (300)

Baupionier-Bataillon 66

Baupionier-Bataillon 146

Baupionier-Bataillon 737

Sicherungs-Bataillon 944 (200)

7 Genesungs-Kompanie (73)

Feldgendarmerie Kompanie 225

Feldgendarmerie Kompanie (mot) 914

Pionier-Sturm-Bataillon 500 (604)

Infanterie-Abteilung Arzberger (630)

Grenadier-Abteilung Benthin (545) –
Major Benthin

Panzergrenadier-Ersatz-Bataillon 5 (572)

Fusilier-Bataillon 73

Grenadier-Abteilung z.b.v. 550 (400)

Grenadier-Abteilung z.b.v. 560 (400)

Panzerabteilung (Fkl) 302 (160), 24 × StuG III –
Major Reinert

Sturmgeschütz-Ersatz-Abteilung 200 (160) –
Major Rupert Gruber

Panzer Sturm-Morser Kompanie 1000 (56)

Sturmpanzer-Kompanie z.b.v. 218 (78) –
Hauptmann Kellmann

Panzer Ausbildung Zug 5

Schwere Stellungs-Werfer-Batterie 201 (64)

Artillerie-Abteilung 507 (76),
6 × 105mm 1.FH 18

Eisb. Panzerzug 75 (49) – Hauptmann
Franz Edon

(1 Battery) Schwere Artillerie-Abteilung 154,
4 × 150mm s.FH 18

2 Schwere Artillerie-Abteilung 641,
2 × 305mm mortars

1 Battery of 2 × 210mm Mortars

Heeres Artillerie Batterie 638, 60cm 'Ziu' (113)

Eisb. Artillerie Batterie 686, 38cm 'Siegfried'

Pionier-Sturm-Bataillon 501

Flammenwerfer-Bataillon Krone (326)

Pionier-Sturm-Regiment 'Herzog' –
Major Herzog

Heeres-Sturmpionier-Bataillon 46 (614) –
Major Wollenberg

Pionier-Bataillon 627 (mot.) (737)

Sicherungs-Regiment 608 (618) – Oberst
Wilhelm Schmidt

Sicherungs-Bataillon 350

Police

Kommandantur Polizei – SS-Brigadeführer Paul Otto Geibel
SS-Polizei-Regiment 22 (800) – Oberst Wilhelm Rodewald
Reserve-Polizei Kompanie (220)
SA-Standarte 'Feldherrhalle' (200)
Gendarmerie (250) – Oberst Gode
Ordnungspolizei (150)
Sicherheitspolizei (SD) (150) – SS-Standartenführer Ludwig Hahn

Hilfs. Polizeiabteilung 21 'Sarnow'
Polizeiabteilung 'Burkhardt' (376)
Eisb. Polizei-Kompanie Walter' (271)
I/Polizei-Schützen-Regiment 35
Polizei Wacht Bataillon 'Warschau' (166)
SD-Kompanie 'Warschau'
SD-Kompanie 'Poznan'
Feuerschütz Polizeiabteilung 96 (mot.) (202)
Polizei Geschütze-Battalion, 4 × 76.2mm Russian guns
Landesschützen-Battalion 246 (341)

Waffen-SS

Kosaken Kompanie (150)
2 × SS Feldersatz Abteilungen
SS-Panzergrenadier Ersatz-Abteilung 3 – Obersturmführer Martin Patz
SS-Reitersturm 8 (200) – Hauptsturmführer Dichtmann
SS-Sonderregiment Dirlewanger (881) – SS-Standartenführer Oskar Dirlewanger
1st Regiment/Waffen-Sturm-Brigade RONA (Kaminski Brigade) (1,585) – Sturmbannführer Ivan Frolov
3/5S-Flak-Regiment 'Wiking'
SS-Jager-Abteilung 501 (461)
Grenadier Kompanie, SS-Junkerschule Treskau
Kampfgruppe der SS-Führerschule Braunschweig
SS-Kompanie (gem.), Warschau
Schwere SS-Kompanie Rontgen-Posen (200)
SS-Kavallerie-Ersatz-Abteilung

III/SS-Polizei-Regiment 17
III/SS-Polizei-Regiment 23
Abwehr-Abteilung D – SD-Hauptsturmführer Spilker
I and III Ostmuselmannische 55-Regiment (550)
Aserbaidschanische Feld-Bataillon 1/III (657) – Hauptmann Werner Scharrenberg
II Gebirgsjäger-Regiment 'Bergmann' (Azerbaijani) (556) – Hauptmann Hubert Mertelsmann
Russische Reiter-Abteilung 580
Reiter-Abteilung 3/Kosaken
Sicherungs-Regiment 57 (944)
Kosaken-Abteilung 69 (773)
Kosaken-Abteilung 572 (619)
Kosaken-Abteilung 579
Kosaken-Abteilung 960
Kosaken-Reiter-Regiment 3 (660)

Luftwaffe

Feldersatz-Bataillon (FEB)
Heeres Artillerie Batterie 428, 2 × 60cm Rex, Thor
19 Panzer Division:
Panzergrenadier-Regiment 73
Panzergrenadier-Regiment 74
Panzer-Aufklärungs-Abteilung 19
Panzer-Artillerie-Regiment 19
Panzerjäger-Abteilung 19
Panzer-Pionier-Bataillon 19
Abteilung 'Schmidt'
Abteilung 'Bernd'

25 Panzer Division
Sturm-Pionier-Bataillon 86
Panzer-Aufklärungs-Abteilung 25
Fallschirm-Panzer Division 1 'Hermann Göring' (800)
Fallschirm-Panzergrenadier-Regiment 2 'Hermann Göring'
I/34 Polizei-Schützen-Regiment – Major Nachtwey
Airport security Okecie (800)
Airport security Bielany (500)
Flak-Regiment 80/Flak-Brigade X (3,000)

Polish Force

AK – Armia Krajowa – Home Army
AL – Armia Ludowa – People's Army
(communists)
OW PPS – Organizacja Wojskowa Polskiej
Partii Socjalistycznej (Military Organizations
Polish Socialist Party)
Group 'Radoslaw' and subdivisions 'KEDYW'
AK 'Zoska' – elite force
AK 'Parasol' – elite force
AK 'Wacek' (2 captured Panthers)
AK 'Broda'

AK 'Czata 49'
AK 'Miotla'
AK 'Piesc' AK 'Wigry'
AK 'Igor' – reserve force, 2nd line
AK 'Hal'
AL – (Communist units ad hoc)
AK 'Pantera'
AK 'Waligora'
AK 'Waga'
AK '1806' (objective to secure Stawki
warehouses)

Notable fighters of the Polish Home Army

Andrzej Łukoski
Ryszard Białous
Andrzej Cielecki
Lidia Daniszewska
Aleksy Dawidowski
Juliusz Bogdan Deczkowski
Jerzy Gawin
Jerzy Jagiełło (porucznik)
Jacek Karpiński
Tadeusz Kosudarski
Jan Kopałka
Jan Rodowicz
Eugeniusz Stasiecki
Krzysztof Kamil Baczyński
Roger Barlet
Henryk Kozłowski
Zygmunt Kujawski
Wacław Micuta

Tadeusz Maślonkowski
Wiktor Matulewicz
Krystyna Niżyńska
Konrad Okolski
Jerzy Ossowski
Jerzy Pepłowski
Anna Wajcowicz
Eugeniusz Romański
Andrzej Romocki
Jan Rossman
Jan J. Więckowski
Tadeusz Sumiński
Kazimierz Wasiłowski
Jerzy Weil
Jan Wuttke
Jan Romocki
Anna Zakrzewska

Notes